If your actions
inspire others
to dream more,
learn more,
do more
and become more,
you are a leader.

John Quincy Adams

To order additional copies of this handbook, or for information on
other WALK THE TALK® products and services,
contact us at
1.888.822.9255
or visit
www.walkthetalk.com

Inspired To Lead

WALK THE TALK books may be purchased for educational, business, or sales
promotion use.

Printed in the United States of America
10 9 8 7 6 5 4 3 2 1

$12.95

ISBN 978-1-935537-69-4

51295>

9 781935 537694

Printed in the United States of America

at MultiAd Inc.

Contents

To my sons, Ryan and Connor;
Persistence is not climbing the mountain –
it is promising yourself
there is no mountain you cannot climb.

To inspire, leaders need to be inspired.

The most effective leaders throughout the ages have always been able to convey to their followers not just critical information but also a driving inspiration. The ability to connect on a deeper level than simply giving orders is what transforms the ordinary into the extraordinary in achieving challenging goals. Tell people where they are going and they may get there; inspire them with why they are going there and they will move mountains.

To inspire, leaders need to be inspired. Skill without motivation is like a Ferrari with no gas. This book is fuel for the journey – a valuable resource that can propel you and your team forward; a collection of empowering, true-life stories that offer the acceleration of inspiration.

Intentionally brief, each vignette is a snapshot of real-world achievement, a testament to people whose lives, actions and commitment left a mark and made a difference. Each narrative is a beacon in the night, lighting a path that leaves us a little more inspired, a bit more focused. These are stories drawn from many venues but each is a unique perspective on the human experience, a celebration of the human spirit and a reminder of the hero inside each of us.

After each vignette is a brief summation of the leadership lessons contained in the story. These insights illuminate the takeaways that transform an inspiring story into a teachable moment. They link a message from yesterday to the needs of today, giving leaders practical tools they can deploy in their journey and a dose of motivation to get there!

Inspired to Lead is evergreen – fresh and inspiring every time you pick it up; no matter how many times you revisit its pages. That's the power that true-life achievement has to motivate and spark success; becoming a wellspring that refreshes both the leader and the team. True inspiration is timeless.

• Inspired to Lead will be a book you keep on your desk, dog-eared and worn from repeated use, a tangible reminder that good leaders not only give motivation but also seek motivation.

• Use it as a burst of inspiration to start your day, share it with a colleague when they need a lift, get copies for your team and integrate the lessons into teaching moments at staff meetings, training sessions or retreats.

• The vignettes are easily adapted to almost any leadership challenge and thus each story becomes a powerful tool you can use as leader, teacher and mentor.

Inspiration is contagious; the more we are exposed to it, the more we inevitably pass it on. Robert Burton once said, "I light my candle from their torches."

Inspiration is meant to be shared, to be passed on, to be a spark that rekindles the best in us. This book is a torch, filled with inspiring moments that invite you to light your leadership candle and leave its pages refreshed, renewed and

Inspired to Lead!

We must not,
in trying to think about
how we can make
a big difference,
ignore the small daily differences
we can make,
which over time,
add up to big differences
that we often
cannot forsee.

Marian Wright Edelman

Lesson 1: The Real Race

On September 14, 2007, Ambassador Nancy G. Brinker was sworn in as Chief of Protocol of the United States. In this role, Ms. Brinker advises, assists and supports the President of the United States, the Vice President and the Secretary of State on official matters of diplomatic procedure. She accompanies the President on official visits abroad and serves as the President's personal representative and liaison to the foreign Ambassadors in Washington. It is a position of significant importance held by a woman who has made achievement seem routine.

Brinker graduated in 1968 from the University of Illinois at Urbana-Champaign, studying broadcast journalism and orchestrating programs for several public relations and marketing firms. That same year, Brinker began a business career by entering the executive training program at Neiman Marcus in Dallas, Texas. In 1994, Brinker founded In Your Corner, Inc., a business venture designed to meet the retail consumer need for reliable health and wellness products and information.

She has served as a director of several publicly held corporations including Manpower, Inc., United Rentals, Inc., U.S. Oncology, Inc., Netmarket, Inc., and the Meditrust Corporation, among others. She is a hard-charger who made things happen and moved up as they did – moved all the way up to an office at 1600 Pennsylvania Avenue.

Viewed through any lens, Nancy Brinker is an extraordinary person who has served her country through several Presidents and numerous challenging, high level positions including an appointment by President Bush to serve as U.S. Ambassador to the Republic of Hungary.

Her list of accolades is stunning and includes Time Magazine's 100 Most Influential People in the World, The Texas Governor's Award for Outstanding National Service, The Jefferson Award for Greatest Public Service by a Private Citizen, the 2007 Castle Connolly "National Health Leadership" Award; Trumpet Foundation's 2007 President's Award, Ladies' Home Journal's 100 Most Important Women of the 20th Century, the Sisters Network 2001 Lifetime Achievement Award, and Biography Magazine's The 25 Most Powerful Women in America.

This is one of the most accomplished professional women in the country.

But this story isn't about one woman's race to the top of the business and government service ladders. It's about one woman's rise from the depths of grief to impact the lives of millions of women (and men) across the world.

You see, while Brinker has reached the pinnacle of public service in the halls of the White House, her greatest contribution came when she made a promise to her dying sister in 1980.

Nancy and Suzy were inseparable growing up in Peoria, Illinois. Suzy, the older sister, was the high school homecoming queen and college beauty queen while Nancy was always the tomboy and mischief-maker. As they grew and married, Brinker moved to Dallas while Suzy stayed in Peoria. The two sisters called each other almost every afternoon to catch up on the day's events and share some laughs.

But one day, the laughter was replaced with shock when news came that Suzy had breast cancer.

Suzy battled bravely, often with Nancy at her side, but three years after her diagnosis, Suzy died at the age of 36 – but not before she asked

Nancy for something very important. Suzy left Nancy with a mission –
extracting a promise from her younger sis (who she had always admired
for her get-it-done spirit) that Nancy would do everything in her power
to help other women fight this terrible disease.

It is a promise that Nancy kept.

In fact, it is one she threw herself into and millions of women are the
better for her extraordinary efforts. Today, the Susan G. Komen for
the Cure Foundation is recognized as the nation's leading catalyst in
the fight against breast cancer, boasting more than 100,000 volunteers
working through a network of 125 U.S. and international affiliates. The
Susan G. Komen for the Cure's signature program - the Race for the
Cure, is the largest series of 5K run/fitness walks in the world.

Since its origin in 1983 in Dallas, Texas, the Race for the Cure Series
has grown from one local race with 800 participants to a national series
of 112 races with over a million participants. The Foundation has
become an institutional icon whose funding has literally changed the
landscape of cancer research, treatment options and public awareness of
one of the most feared diseases in the world.

To learn more:
Susan G. Komen for the Cure Foundation
www.Komen.org

One woman making a difference for millions…because she kept a promise.

Keep even small commitments. The reason is clear – there is potential for greatness in every promise, every commitment. When we keep those promises, we unleash that potential and the results can be life changing.

Nancy Brinker is a powerful example that leadership is taking action, not taking bows. Leaders are not afraid to act even when the full ramifications of their decisions may not be known. They understand that paralysis-of-analysis is more of an impediment to success than having to make adjustments to imperfect actions.

Faced with challenging circumstances, it is almost always better to do something than do nothing since the fact that you acted exposes options, ideas or opportunities that did not exist or were not visible before.

Brinker could not have known that her first Race for the Cure would eventually swell to more than a million participants but she didn't have to – all she needed to know was that it was a viable first step in keeping her promise to her sister.

What first steps do you need to take?

Take the step. Get started. Don't wait. Act on what you know and move in the direction you need to go.

Leaders realize that there is power in a promise and courage in commitment and that only in working for something greater than ourselves can we reach our full leadership potential.

Many years from now, no one will remember that Nancy Brinker was the first person to officially greet Pope Benedict XVI when he landed in the United States or many other important but fleeting moments on her impressive resume – but countless women will live to have their own successes, families and futures because of the work done by the Susan G. Komen Foundation – an organization that exists only because one woman kept her promise.

Sometimes our light goes out but
is blown into flame
by another human being.
Each of us
owes deepest thanks
to those who have
rekindled this light.

Albert Schweitzer

Lesson 2: Leadership in a Bucket

John Foglesong is not a famous athlete, successful entrepreneur, high profile politician, gifted writer, inspiring speaker, innovative educator or heroic serviceman. He is not wealthy – at least in terms of material possessions – and he is certainly not likely to become so anytime soon. In fact, most of John's life has been an abysmal failure.

For most of the past 30 years, John has been in prison or in trouble. He was a petty thief who stole to support a drug habit that consumed and destroyed his youth. Driven by an addiction he could not control, John fell from one miserable circumstance to the next. He knows what homelessness is; having slept for years in makeshift shelters in parks, under bridges, on heating grates, in doorways or wherever he could sleep off his hangover or come down from a drug induced high.

If life is a journey, John has stumbled through most of his invisible.

But lives change. People change. How and why are less important than the fact that they change. John changed. Faced with the utter collapse of his life and the certainty of an early death if he did not find a new path, the fifty-something hobo made a life altering commitment – to himself – and everyday now he is grateful for that new beginning.

"Being thankful is not simply something we say, it's something we do", John says as he reflects on his climb out of despair. John puts his gratitude in action right where he spent much of the past three decades—in prison and on the streets of Salem, Oregon.

On most Fridays, you can find John in prison – as a visitor now instead of a resident. He holds a 12-step meeting for inmates trying to break their own cycle of addiction and despair. On Sundays after church, he and his wife, Deana, are regulars in Marion Square Park, giving away food, clothing, and shoes to anyone who needs them. There is no paperwork or fanfare, no press coverage or program; just John and his wife distributing whatever they have to share with people who have nothing to give and no one to care.

But John takes care of that last need too, sharing his own remarkable recovery from the destructive cycle of drug addiction, petty crime, and homelessness with those who have not yet found their way out of the darkness. He never gets tired of telling people: "I know what you're going through. I lived it for thirty years. You don't have to stay stuck. If you're serious about changing your life and willing to do the work, I'm here to give you a hand."

John has helped homeless addicts find recovery programs, housing, jobs, and ways to take better care of their families.

How does he fund this generosity?

He is not CEO of any foundation, not an executive of any national agency or community outreach program. He does not have Hollywood donors or apply for federal grants. No, John just makes what he has stretch. He funds his outreach work with the modest $20,000 annual income from his window-washing business.

That's right, John washes windows.

He started with $25 worth of squeegees, buckets, and towels and went door to door, business to business offering to clean windows for a few dollars. Now he has 80 clients – not an empire by any means but a business nonetheless, one he is proud of and one that delivers more to the bottom-line than debits and credits.

John built a business but answered a calling. He washes windows but his real joy comes from the opportunity to change lives.

"You help one person, and pretty soon they're helping someone else. You never know how many people you've touched just by reaching out to one."

I doubt there is a more pure definition of success.

Lessons For Leaders

There are leaders of multi-billion dollar corporations who could learn a lot about leadership from one man with a bucket and a squeegee.

The stewardship that John displays in making room inside a $20,000 annual income for not just himself and his wife but for countless strangers in need puts the excesses and recklessness of many corporate high rollers to shame. John's ability to multiply his impact through little more than a relentless personal commitment to make what he has stretch farther than it should is a testament to the fact that fiscal discipline is not the magic of Wharton School wizardry.

> You do not have to be a Harvard MBA to understand good business practices; you just have to lead with a purpose and act with integrity.

But John's leadership lessons for us go much deeper than the balance sheet. His life is validation that we are never too far gone to turn the corner. John's transformation is remarkable and inspiring not because he found fame and fortune but because he didn't.

John's story reminds us that success in business should be a means to an end, not an end in itself; that what we do for a living should not define what we do for a life.

His impact as an agent of change in the lives of other people far exceeds his business prowess – an example of what true leadership really is, making the most of what we have by multiplying what we are given to benefit more than just ourselves.

John leads by example; turning his own mistakes into lessons that others relate to and learn from; motivating others to discover the hero inside each of us.

The desire to lead by example is one we can all take something from.

On paper, John's resume is one nearly all of us would discard as we screened candidates for employment. Who among us would hire an ex-con, ex-drug addict, ex-homeless man who washes windows as an occupation?

These are not the credentials any of us would consider for more than a few seconds – and yet, were we to judge on paper alone we would miss an extraordinary individual who knows more about change than any consultant we ever hired and who could teach our management more than a few things about leadership ... starting with how to care about the people you lead.

Those are certainly lessons worth learning.

If you can't feed
a hundred people,
then just feed
one.

Mother Teresa

Lesson 3: Brown Bag Leadership

One of my favorite stories came to me by email from a friend who wrote...

I put my carry-on in the luggage compartment and sat down in my assigned seat. It was going to be a long flight so I was glad to have a good book to read. Perhaps, I will even get a short nap, I thought to myself. Just before take-off, a line of soldiers came down the aisle and filled all the vacant seats, totally surrounding me. I decided to start a conversation.

"Where are you headed?" I asked the soldier seated nearest to me. "Chicago - to Great Lakes Base; we'll be there for two weeks for special training, and then we're being deployed to Iraq."

After flying for about an hour, an announcement was made that sack lunches were available for five dollars. It would be several hours before we reached Chicago, and I quickly decided a lunch would help pass the time. As I reached for my wallet, I overheard one of the soldiers ask his buddy if he planned to buy lunch.

"No, that seems like a lot of money for just a sack lunch. Probably wouldn't be worth five bucks. I'll wait till we get to Chicago." His friend agreed. I looked around at the other soldiers. None were buying lunch.

I walked to the back of the plane and handed the flight attendant a fifty dollar bill. "Please take a lunch to all those soldiers."

She grabbed my arms and squeezed tightly. Her eyes wet with tears, she thanked me, "My son is a soldier in Iraq; it's almost like you are doing it for him."

Picking up ten sacks, she headed up the aisle to where the soldiers were seated. She stopped at my seat and asked, "Which do you like best - beef or chicken?" "Chicken," I replied, wondering why she asked. She turned and went to the front of plane, returning a minute later with a dinner plate from first class. "This is yours, thanks."

After we finished eating, I went again to the back of the plane, to stretch my legs. A man stopped me. "I saw what you did. I want to be part of it. Here, take this." He handed me twenty-five dollars.

Soon after I returned to my seat, the Flight Captain came down the aisle. When he got to my row he stopped, smiled, held out his hand, and said, "I want to shake your hand." With a booming voice he said, "I was a soldier too - a military pilot. Once, someone bought me a lunch. It was an act of kindness that I never forgot." I was embarrassed when applause was heard from all of the passengers.

Later I walked to the front of the plane to again stretch my legs. A man who was seated about six rows in front of me reached out his hand, wanting to shake mine. He left another twenty-five dollars in my palm.

When we landed in Chicago I gathered my belongings and started to deplane. Waiting just inside the airplane door was a man who stopped me, put something in my shirt pocket, turned, and walked away without saying a word. Another twenty-five dollars!

Upon entering the terminal, I saw the soldiers gathering for their trip to the base. I walked over to them and handed them the seventy-five dollars that people had given to me.

"It will take you some time to reach the base and I'm sure you may want another sandwich along the way. Be safe and Godspeed."

A veteran is someone who, at one point in his or her life, wrote a blank check made payable to "The United States of America" for an amount of "up to and including my life."

Ten young men were headed into harm's way for our country and all I could give them were a couple of meals. It seemed so little, but I was wrong.

A moment after I left them, a voice called out, "Sir!"

I turned back and there in the middle of the main walkway, amid a crush of travelers, 10 of our nation's finest stood at attention, looking me straight in the eyes and rendering the crispest salutes I have ever seen.

This is a story about seeing a leadership moment in the most ordinary of situations. It's a story about how lunch for a few strangers grows into a leadership experience that ripples far beyond the bounds of one simple act. This is a story that illustrates one of the bedrock truisms of leadership:

Managers act when given an opportunity. Leaders make an opportunity to act.

The distinction is powerful and at the core of what differentiates leaders from managers. It does not diminish the value of a manager to say that a leader views opportunity through more agile eyes; it simply recognizes leadership for what it is – the embodiment of Hannibal's, "We will find a way, or make one."

Leaders identify situations where they can make a difference and then step boldly into those environments, taking action without hesitation. Effective leaders do not need or even seek permission or approval from others to act in settings where their presence would be of immediate benefit.

Leaders don't bounce off the obvious or wait to see if anyone else is onboard with what they know needs done – if it is the right thing to do, they do it. Leaders do not fear walking that line between confident intervention and reckless interference. Value-driven decisions come easily to the leader.

Leadership also inspires others to become involved. One man buying a few lunches on an airplane sets in motion a wave of goodwill.

The very essence of a leader is someone who, by example, motivates others to join the cause or engage the moment to make something positive happen.

People are willing to participate in meaningful activities but many of them need a catalyst, a trigger, a primer to unleash that participation.

In science, Newton's First Law says that a body at rest tends to stay at rest unless acted on by an outside force. That's true with people too. Leaders offer that "push" that gets others going; they are the "outside force" that instigates action.

What situations need a "push" from you?

Leadership is that spark that multiplies the bounty of the harvest.

Good leaders leverage their presence so their impact is not additive but exponential. Leadership takes one action and causes a chain reaction that spreads rapidly and forcefully. The result is an outcome that would have been impossible for one but is attainable with many. The desired goal is not met, it is exceeded.

This story isn't about buying lunch for ten hungry soldiers. It's about nourishing a need we have as leaders to do what is right when we know the moment is at hand to make a difference.

Get started!

Energy and persistence
conquer all things.

Benjamin Franklin

Lesson 4: Beyond Gold

Wilma was born prematurely on June 23, 1940, weighing just 4 1/2 pounds, the 20th of her father Ed's 22 children (from two marriages). She would grow up poor in St. Bethlehem, Tennessee, surrounded by segregation and prejudice – but seeds of greatness were already planted in this most unlikely of heroes.

Stricken almost from birth with a series of debilitating illnesses, this future champion spent the majority of her childhood in bed where the sickly girl suffered from double pneumonia, scarlet fever, whooping cough, measles and chicken pox. The final indignity came when she contracted polio at age 6, losing the use of her left leg and forcing her to wear metal leg braces.

Was this the profile of a future Olympian? Hardly. But Wilma Rudolf would grow up to change not just sports but hearts and minds the world over. On legs once too weak to stand, she would become "the fastest woman in the world" and the first American woman to win 3 gold medals in one Olympics.

From a body once so weak that it lay in bed for most of its youth, a champion would emerge who would be voted into the Black Athletes Hall of Fame and the National Track and Field Hall of Fame. From one of the most humble, unassuming personalities comes a giant of change and inspiration.

Wilma loved sports and despite the braces on her legs dreamed of playing. "When you come from a large, wonderful family, there's always a way to achieve your goals," Wilma said, so together the family faced the hardship. Her brothers and sisters took turns massaging the youngster's crippled leg every day and once a week her mother, Blanche, a domestic worker, drove her 90 miles roundtrip to a Nashville hospital for therapy.

By age 9, Wilma was freed of the metal leg braces. She immediately started playing basketball with a passion. In high school, she made the girls basketball team, earning all-state honors and setting a state scoring record with 49 points in one game.

But it was Ed Temple, Tennessee State's women's track coach, who saw something else in Wilma that he knew was special – speed. Temple inspired Wilma; she attended his track team practices even while she was finishing high school and excelled under his tutelage. In 1960, she was selected to join America's track team for the Olympic Games in Rome.

On that world stage, Wilma won the 100 meter, 200 meter and anchored the 4x100 meter relay team, earning 3 gold medals, setting records and endearing herself to legions of fans. The press called her, "The Black Pearl" or "The Black Gazelle" and marveled at her speed. "I don't know why I run so fast," she once said, "I just run." But she did more than run; she promoted her country, tore down barriers and in her soft-spoken, gracious manner, paved the way for African-American athletes who came later.

Back home, her achievements opened minds as well. When Wilma returned from the Rome Olympics, Tennessee Gov. Buford Ellington, elected as "an old-fashioned segregationist," planned to head her victory celebration. But Wilma would have no part of a segregated celebration so her parade and banquet became the first integrated events in her hometown of Clarksville.

In her post-Olympic years, she worked as a track coach at Indiana's DePauw University and served as a U.S. goodwill ambassador to French West Africa but she said her greatest accomplishment was creating the Wilma Rudolph Foundation, a not-for-profit, community-based amateur sports program.

"I tell them (young people) that the most important aspect is to be yourself and have confidence in yourself," she said.

"I remind them the triumph can't be had without the struggle."

Rudolph died of brain cancer at age 54 leaving a legacy of speed, grace and the heights to which one can soar when we push past our limitations and unleash the hero we each have inside.

"The triumph can't be had without the struggle" ... what a superb insight that is for us as leaders.

Leadership is not easy. It is not without setbacks, hardships and even failure. Circumstances are often not ideal, resources inadequate, timelines mercilessly restrictive. In our quest to achieve meaningful goals, we frequently struggle to establish, let alone maintain, momentum.

But these times of distress are precisely those that shape a leader. In calm seas and fair winds, no ship needs a captain; but churn the water, howl the wind and let loose the tempest and those with the mettle to lead rise to the challenge. Struggle is the price of progress, a toll the intrepid pay in full if they are to lead their team to achievement.

"Conquering Adversity" reminds leaders that adversity is never a question of if, only a matter of when, so we must prepare ourselves and our team. We must anticipate adversity and communicate to our team our strategies, tactics and positive attitude so they share our confidence to meet even the most demanding crisis. Leaders know that anything worth doing will require unyielding perseverance.

Paul Woodside, a noted football coach and leadership expert, is fond of saying, *"big dreams should never come easy."*

He's right – the road to the top never runs downhill.

Leaders need to see not just the big picture but the right picture. Today's limitations do not have to be tomorrow's realities.

Wilma Rudolf did not allow years of physical disability to define her infinite possibility. She wanted to be in a position to excel when her circumstances changed - so she used her times of struggle to strengthen not just her legs but her desire, her dreams and her goals.

In our work, do we stay mired in the disability of the moment or do we free ourselves to see the possibilities of tomorrow? Leaders replace frustration with preparation; setback with vision; failure with drive.

Champions leave a legacy larger than their victories; winners become legends when their impact reverberates far beyond the record books, podiums or arenas; and heroes lead not just their teams but their times. Wilma was a pioneer for African-American athletes, especially women, but she was more than that – she broke barriers, not just records; she touched lives and lifted others up. Leaders do that because they know their actions impact circles far wider than their immediate colleagues.

Accomplishment is winning your gold medal – leadership is inspiring others to win theirs.

Growing up poor, sickly, crippled and disadvantaged gave Wilma Rudolf every excuse to fail – or every reason to soar. She chose the latter and in the process illuminated a lesson in leadership for all of us.

Once you choose hope,
anything is possible.

Christopher Reeves

Lesson 5: No Losers

They played one of the most memorable high school football games in history in the fall of 2008 in Grapevine, Texas. It was Grapevine Faith vs. Gainesville State School and everything about it was upside down. For instance, when Gainesville State came out to take the field, the Grapevine Faith fans made a 40-yard spirit line for them to run through. That's right, hometown fans made a spirit line for the visiting team.

The Grapevine fans even made a banner for Gainesville players to crash through at the end. It said, "Go Tornadoes!" Which is also weird, because Faith is the Lions. More than 200 Faith fans sat on the Gainesville side and kept cheering the Gainesville players on—by name.

"I never in my life thought I'd hear people cheering for us," recalls Gainesville's QB and middle linebacker, Isaiah.

And even though Faith walloped Gainesville, 33-14, the Gainesville kids were so happy that after the game they gave their head coach, Mark Williams, a sideline squirt-bottle shower like he'd just won a state title. It has to be the first Gatorade bath in history for a coach with an 0-9 record.

But with the game over, everyone could see 12 uniformed officers escorting the 14 Gainesville players off the field. They lined the players up in groups of five—handcuffs ready in their back pockets—and marched them to the team bus. That's because Gainesville is a maximum-security correctional facility 75 miles north of Dallas. Every game it plays is on the road.

This all started when Faith's head coach, Kris Hogan, wanted to do something kind for the Gainesville team. Faith had never played Gainesville, but he already knew the score. Faith was 7-2 going into the game, Gainesville 0-8 with 2 touchdowns all year. Faith has 70 kids on the roster, 11 coaches, the latest equipment and involved parents. Gainesville has a lot of kids with convictions for drugs, assault and robbery—many of whose families had disowned them—wearing 7 year-old shoulder pads and ancient helmets.

So Hogan had this idea. What if half of our fans—for one night only—cheered for the other team? He sent out an email asking people to do just that. "Here's the message I want you to send:" Hogan wrote.

"You are just as valuable as any other person on planet Earth."

Some people were naturally confused. One Faith player walked into Hogan's office and asked, "Coach, why are we doing this?" And Hogan said, "Imagine if you didn't have a home life. Imagine if everybody had pretty much given up on you. Now imagine what it would mean for hundreds of people to suddenly believe in you."

And so, on that night, the Gainesville Tornadoes turned around on their bench to see something they never had before - hundreds of fans and actual cheerleaders! It was a strange experience for boys who most people would cross the street to avoid. "These people, they were yellin' for us! By our names!" said Alex, a Gainesville lineman. Maybe it figures that Gainesville played better than it had all season, scoring the game's last two touchdowns.

After the game, both teams gathered in the middle of the field to pray and that's when Isaiah surprised everybody by asking to lead. "We had no idea what the kid was going to say," remembers Coach Hogan.

But Isaiah said this: "Lord, I don't know how this happened, so I don't know how to say Thank You, but I never would've known there was so many people in the world that cared about us." And it was a good thing everybody's heads were bowed because they might have seen Hogan wiping away tears.

As the Tornadoes walked back to their bus under guard, they each were handed a bag for the ride home—a burger, some fries, a soda, some candy, a Bible and an encouraging letter from a Faith player.

The Gainesville coach saw Hogan, grabbed him hard by the shoulders and said, "You'll never know what your people did for these kids tonight. You'll never, ever know."

And as the bus pulled away, all the Gainesville players crammed to one side and pressed their hands to the window, staring at these people they'd never met before, watching their waves and smiles disappearing into the night.

"You are just as valuable as any other person on planet Earth."

The leadership lessons in that one statement are as profound as any we might encounter in a dozen best-selling business books. Perhaps more so, because the intended recipients of that message were young men who before this game may never have experienced that sense of value or even believed in their own self-worth. Certainly, they were a group that had never received so valuable a gift from complete strangers.

But one man's leadership sparked actions that led an entire community to rally behind kids who no one had ever supported; the leader of one team became the model for every team.

How powerful a message do we send as leaders when we proclaim the intrinsic value of every member of our team? And how much greater is that message when we extend that belief even to those we oppose with respect?

The inspiration of Coach Hogan's leadership in this game was that he didn't just lead his team to victory; he created a situation where there were no losers. His leadership transcended the game and made a difference on levels far deeper than the scoreboard.

In the end, Coach Hogan's players understood how fortunate they were for the life they had, his assistant coaches saw firsthand that they could have an impact far beyond the field, the opposing players experienced a sense of belonging and support that they could not have imagined, the opposing coach shared a depth of gratitude for a gesture he could never have expected his team to receive, and a community discovered the pure joy of cheering for someone who has never heard a kind voice raised on their behalf.

So many lessons from one humble act of leadership.

As leaders, we need to believe that every person has value and that one of our responsibilities is to find ways to lift people up even when others discard them. Leadership is creating opportunities that transcend the moment; opportunities where your example can inspire not just direct; opportunities where the benefits of your actions spill over the boundaries of your span of control.

In "doing our job" let's not limit the impact of our efforts or see the ultimate measure of our success as wins and losses.

As a leader, let's recognize that it's a different game when you coach the outcome not just the score. Leading the favored is easy; championing the outcast takes courage.

Winning has many faces – even ones you may never know.

Life takes on meaning
when you
become motivated,
set goals,
and charge after them
in an unstoppable manner.

Les Brown

Lesson 6: Whispered Dreams

You may not know Monty Roberts by name; but you know of Monty Roberts.

Horses were Monty's life as a young boy. At age 13, on a trip to Nevada to round up wild Mustangs for a rodeo, Monty became captivated by the animals, endlessly observing their behavior and interactions. His father was an itinerant horse trainer, who scratched out a humble living traveling from farm to farm, stable to stable looking for whatever work was available. But despite this poor, nomadic childhood that uprooted him from school after school, Monty had a clear vision of the direction he wanted for his life.

One of his defining moments as a young man, one that challenged his dreams, came as a senior in high school when a teacher gave him a homework assignment to write a paper about what he wanted to do when he grew up. Monty wrote what he was convinced was a 7-page masterpiece detailing how he wanted to own a 200-acre ranch where he could raise horses. He sketched the position of every building, the track, the stables and even details of a 4,000 square foot home.

This was his dream; a dream as real, clear and powerful in his mind's eye as any motivation the young man could imagine. With great enthusiasm and excitement, he turned in his paper. The paper came back to Monty marked with a bright red, "F", and a note to see the teacher after class.

The teacher chastised Monty, "This is an unrealistic dream for a young boy like you. You have no money. You come from an itinerant family. You have no resources. Owning a horse ranch requires a lot of money ...

There's no way you could ever do it," The teacher told Monty to rewrite the paper with a "more realistic goal" and he would reconsider his grade. Monty went home and thought about it long and hard for one week. Finally, after contemplating the paper and his teacher's admonishment, the boy turned back in the same paper, making no changes save one brief comment,

"You can keep the 'F', and I'll keep my dream."

Monty's courage of commitment did more than keep his dream – it fueled his pursuit of it and set the stage for a remarkable and successful life. You might know Monty by another name, "The Horse Whisperer." He was the inspiration behind Robert Redford's acclaimed movie and became famous for his Join-Up® technique that "breaks" wild or traumatized horses through non-violent techniques. Monty uses body language and soft words to gain the animal's trust and invite a desired response. He is literally a world-wide phenomenon with admirers that include no less than the Queen of England.

The kid with the failing grade is also a best-selling author with 5 books and millions of readers. He and his wife have three children and have been foster parents to 47 others. He established a horse training academy based on his special techniques, offers youth camps and is active in numerous charitable organizations. Oh, and Monty's ranch? Yes, not surprisingly, he has a 200-acred horse ranch in San Ysidro, California with a beautiful complex of buildings, pastures and tracks built just as he laid it out back at age 17.

He also has that 4,000 square foot home; and in the great room, hanging over the fireplace mantle where it commands the attention of everyone who enters, is a framed, 7-page high school paper, still marked with that blazing red "F."

Monty Roberts faced a choice. He could rewrite his dreams to fit someone else's expectations or he could cling to his dream and accept the short term setback of that commitment. In refusing to limit his own potential because of the adversity of his youth or the pessimism of his teacher, Monty practiced one of the underlying principals in my "Conquering Adversity" message – "never trade tomorrow's dreams for yesterday's nightmares."

At the heart of being a leader is having the courage of your own convictions, especially when those convictions are challenged, chastised or threatened. Always stand on your values and move in the direction of your dreams.

In our role as leaders, we are stewards of not just our own goals but also the goals and aspirations of those we lead. We must become champions of other people's dreams as well. Effective leaders cultivate, support and celebrate the heights those with whom they work and interact are trying to reach. They are not intimidated by other's success; they facilitate it.

Leaders do not fear losing talent; they fear wasting potential and so they promote, grow and groom each team member – taking pride in the ever increasing contributions of those who stubbornly refuse to yield their dreams.

We must be a force for optimism and persistence in those who are striving to be and do more – lifting up those around us; sharing skills and providing opportunities for growth and advancement. Leadership is more than hitting a number on paper; it's hitting the mark in someone's life.

Dreams are wishes with an action plan – so act. Have the courage to commit to your goals even when others discourage or reject your vision; and have the strength of character to help others do the same. It starts with commitment.

Nobody can make you
feel inferior
without your consent.

Eleanor Roosevelt

Lesson 7: Elephants

One day a grandmother took her grandson to the circus. They watched the performers and sat mesmerized by all the exotic animals but by far the one animal that captured the imagination of the little boy more than any other was the elephants. They were enormous and yet moved so gracefully. They were so strong and yet had a gentle touch in the way they interacted with their keepers. They were smart and quite brave; never showing any signs of being afraid even when the tigers were in the same ring. The elephants were remarkable creatures, and the boy wanted so badly to get even closer to them.

After a long day, the grandmother and grandson were walking slowly toward the exit when they cut behind one of the big top tents. As they rounded some crates, both stopped in their tracks and stared into the eyes of 5 adult elephants calmly eating piles of hay. The beasts paused for a moment and then continued curling one mouthful of hay after another with their long trunks. The boy was frozen in awe – the elephants seemed twice as big up close as they had in the ring.

A moment later, a man appeared from behind one of the elephants carrying a bucket and broom. Seeing the boy and his grandmother, he introduced himself and said his job was to keep the elephants clean and fed but that the two surprise visitors were welcome to stay a moment.

The little boy could not contain himself. He asked how old the elephants were, how much they weighed, what they liked to eat, did they ever get tired and on and on and on.

The keeper answered every question.

Then the boy noticed the rope around a back leg of each of the elephants. The rope was tied to a steel spike driven into the ground but next to the gigantic grey shapes it seemed like simple yarn.

The boy asked the keeper how could that tiny rope holds back such a huge animal – couldn't the elephants just break the rope and run free?

The keeper smiled at the observant lad and said yes the elephants were strong enough to snap that rope with one tug. The boy wondered out loud then why didn't the elephants do that; why didn't' they break free from something that held them back?

The keeper explained that when the elephants are young they are not as strong so the ropes are able to hold them in place. The young elephant will tug and pull and try to free itself from the tether, but keepers make sure that the ropes are always too strong for the young elephant to break.

The elephants grow up believing that a rope on their back leg is too strong for them to snap so eventually they stop trying.

Even after they grow to a size and strength where they could easily break the rope, they don't because in their mind they believe the rope to be stronger.

That's the power of your mind the grandmother explained to the young boy. What you believe is what you achieve. The elephants could break free of the rope holding them back if they only realized how strong they were, but they remember failing when they were young and they never try again.

Thanking the keeper for his time and courtesy, the grandmother and grandson walked away toward home still talking about those elephants and how they were really stronger than they knew.

There's a bit of elephant in all of us at times.

Business icon, Mary Kay Ash, said, "If you think you can't, you're right." For better or for worse, we are programmable creatures. What we believe is what we achieve – or from another angle, what we believe we can't do is what we will never do. What we accomplish on the outside all starts on the inside.

The elephant is one of the most intelligent animals on the planet, and yet it is easily conditioned at a young age to associate a rope around its leg with an inability to break free. It learns it cannot do something and so it believes it cannot ever do that action even when its abilities have outgrown its limitation. It is easy to become products of our past especially when that past has limited us or held us back.

It's important to ask ourselves from time to time if we are still tethered to things that we have long since outgrown – are we limited now simply because we believe something to be true that is not?

In the course of our lives, we encounter many voices. Some are positive, uplifting, encouraging and empowering – they help us to grow and reach and dream. But sometimes there are negative voices that chide us, degrade us, diminish us; that focus on our failures, reinforce our shortcomings; highlight our inadequacies. Sometimes those voices are loud and repeated or from people we care about or respect and the impact on our lives can be significant.

There are those who elevate themselves by suppressing others with consequences that linger long afterward. These voices of doom and gloom become the rope that holds us in our place, the stake that keeps us tethered to what we could not once do – and a tie that threatens to keep us there because we do not have the courage to believe otherwise.

Leadership is not about cutting the ropes that hold other people back – it's about showing them that they already have the power to free their own potential. Leaders don't do for others what they are incapable of doing for themselves; rather, leaders light the fire inside others that let them see what they are capable of achieving.

It is natural for people to have doubts or to question their abilities or to feel the sting of past failure but the difference between those who succeed and those who stay stagnant comes down to who is willing to persist; who is not afraid to continually test the strength of new skills and the boundaries of new possibilities.

We are indeed stronger than we know and more capable than we realize.

As leaders, it's about believing in that inner hero and not allowing that which tethered us in the past to hold us back from tomorrow's bright promises.

Step up, step out and stretch the limits of your potential.

It is not the oath
that makes us
believe the man,
but the man
the oath.

Aeschylus

Lesson 8: The Promise

Let me begin with an excerpt from my book, <u>Conquering Adversity</u>:

> "After Cynthia's death, there were many days that I did not want to go to work because I was grieving my loss. No one would have denied me my retreat. No one would have criticized my pain, and no one would have begrudged me a day of abdicating my responsibilities. But the days that I wanted to retreat were the days the son taught the father a lesson in the power of persistence.
>
> I put Ryan on the bus for school each morning, and that picture fortified me when my strength waned. I remembered Ryan climbing on the bus each morning and turning to me with a smile and a wave. I remembered his face staring at me through the bus window as it pulled away – a face that carried both pain and hope as he searched to see if I was still waving, as if that reassured him that today would be alright.
>
> His loss was as great as mine, his burden heavier, and yet he persisted. If Ryan could get on that bus each morning, carrying this burden at nine years old, then I could drive to the office and be a professional.
>
> The power of persistence isn't something you learn as you age. It's something you master as you mature – a lesson taught to me by a hero so young."

Ryan turned 20 years old and it was an epiphany for me. It had been over ten years since I had to tell him the unbearable news that his mom had died; ten years since I heard him scream in agony and bolt in fear; ten years since we lived a nightmare no one should endure. It was over ten years ago that a scared little boy asked if we could walk home from the friend's house we were at when I told him about his mom. I can still feel his hand squeezing mine tightly as we made our way at dusk in a light summer rain, the drops mixing with tears as father and son walked slowly home.

It was just past St. Francis Xavier Church as we turned down South Street when Ryan looked up at me and asked, "Dad, will we be alright?" His question pierced my heart and I hoped my own pain was not visible as I answered, "Yes, son, we will be alright. We have each other so I'm sure mom knows we will be alright."

We walked on. We had not quite reached Flower Lane when that face looked up at me again and said,

"I'm going to make my mom proud, Dad. I promise, I'm going to make mom very proud."

He hugged me tightly and I him.

Ten years later, Ryan has surely kept his promise.

He kept his promise because he never gave up. Ryan fought through grief, pain, depression, anger and every negative emotion that comes with a life shattered – but he refused to yield his future to the despair of his past. He didn't stop caring about school; he cared more. He didn't stop being an athlete; he worked harder at it. He didn't withdraw from life; he savored it. He didn't lament lost dreams; he dreamt new ones. He didn't lower the bar for himself; he raised it.

The journey wasn't easy, it wasn't without mistakes and missteps, it demanded that he grow up faster because life had dealt him a tough hand. But he did not quit – not at what he did and not on who he was.

Ryan's dream coming out of high school was to attend Syracuse University and to make the football team as a place kicker. He made that dream a reality and surpassed it. He is the picture of persistence and his future is as bright as his smile. But that success isn't why he kept his promise.

At age 9, he could not have fully understood that what he committed to was not what he would do … it was who he would become. His promise was about his character. He could not have known how the experience would shape his life, sharpen his core values and build from those ruins a foundation that is strong and unshakable.

He could not have known these things; he just went out and did them.

I have never seen the power of persistence demonstrated more clearly than in the life of a little boy who stepped on the bus every day despite his pain; and who now as a young man steps up every day as an inspiration to so many … including his dad.

Persistence isn't climbing the mountain – it's promising yourself there is no mountain you cannot climb.

What mountain are you climbing?

What obstacles are you struggling to clear? What challenge is pressing on your ability to lead?

Persistence is purposeful motion. It serves a cause, drives a dream and stretches the possibilities. Persistence is not enduring mindlessly futile tasks. Lemmings are not persistent in their blind trudge off a cliff – they are simply foolish.

Persistence is not motion for motion's sake – it is action with a purpose that does not yield to adversity.

Leadership demands a resilient spirit. How do we adjust to failure? How do we react to error? What response do we offer when the bottom falls out of our reality? These are not idle quandaries. Anyone can steer the boat in calm seas; captains steer it in a gale.

Perspective bolsters persistence. Persistence without perspective is like a blind man building a house. His hammer may drive a few nails but not before it smacks a lot more thumbs! Ryan's persistence came from his perspective – as he grew, he knew what a "bad" day looked like; he had lived one on a scale few can imagine; so ordinary adversity was less intimidating. Where others become consumed in the fear of failure; Ryan knows failure only comes when you refuse to face your fears.

Leaders do the same when tackling a problem. They keep the magnitude of the issue in perspective; frame it within a context that can be managed; examine what went wrong and look for an adjustment that makes sense. Fear of failure has no place in a leader's mindset.

As a leader, your team looks to you for perspective which is why constant communication is so important. Don't assume they see it as you see it. Communicate your assessment of and your commitment to the task at hand. Share progress, even if it seems slight, as that reinforces for the team the perceived benefit of persistent action.

At nine, Ryan taught me about answering the bell just by going to school every day because I knew how much he hurt. It is a lesson I was proud to learn from a son who was keeping a promise.

As a leader, remember to recognize those on your team who "get on the bus every day."

These champions set aside their worries and get things done. Reward those who demonstrate heart and grit; hold them up as role models for those less stout of effort. And never be too proud to learn from your subordinates – wisdom has no age.

So what are you waiting for?

Gather the team and promise yourselves that together there is no mountain you cannot climb!

True heroism is
remarkably sober,
very un-dramatic.
It is not the urge to
surpass all others
at whatever cost,
but the urge to
serve others
at whatever cost.

Arthur Ashe

Lesson 9: Servant Leader

Steve and Daphne Valentine were driving on the interstate two weeks ago returning from New Jersey where they attended the 70th birthday of Steve's father. Traveling north at 7:15 p.m. on Interstate 81 near Binghamton, they noticed a van began moving erratically in front of them. It rolled slowly down the shoulder of the road, before abruptly veering into traffic.

Steve, a safety consultant with an environmental company, was driving when the van lurched out in front of him. He pushed down on the horn, and pulled into the fast lane to pass the van. As they went by, Daphne, looked into the driver's side window. A woman was slumped back in the seat, apparently unconscious. A little girl was holding onto the wheel, blowing the horn with her other hand, and shouting something the Valentines couldn't hear.

Steve had seconds to react.

He pulled his car onto the inside shoulder, along the grassy strip in the middle of the interstate. He jumped out and waited for a few cars to rocket past. Then he sprinted across the I-81 interstate. He ran after the van. It was in drive, but no one was giving it gas so Steve managed to catch up and yank open the door.

He pulled himself in and hit the brakes. Behind the van, another driver pulled over who had already called 911. He and Steve helped the little girl get into the car with Daphne and the Valentine children. Then the two men ran back to see what they could do for the victim. She was not breathing. She had no pulse. They feared the worst.

Police arrived shortly thereafter, felt for a pulse and finding none began using defibrillators to shock the victim's heart and followed with CPR. Moments later, a crew arrived from an ambulance service and paramedics rushed the woman to a nearby hospital.

Steve and Daphne waited behind, with their children and the little girl, until the child's father came and took her home. The Valentines resumed the long ride home where they got a welcome phone call from a sheriff who told them the 49-year-old victim was alive.

What had happened was this. Mother and daughter were on their way home, traveling at interstate speeds, when the mother collapsed. The daughter, age 11, said that she reached over and grabbed the wheel with one hand. With her other hand, she unsnapped her mother's seat belt, which allowed the girl to shove her mother's foot off the gas pedal. The child then did her best to steer the van to the side of the road.

Yet, the brave fifth grader, couldn't reach the brake. Car after car went speeding past. No one looked over as the little girl pushed down the horn, held grimly to the wheel and screamed for help.

Not far away, Steve and Daphne were hurrying along, worried that they might be late to where they thought they should be ... but soon to discover they were right on time for where they needed to be.

Lessons For Leaders

Nothing in this inspiring story of life-saving action surprises me. I know Steve Valentine personally. In fact, I hired him to be part of my team when I was head of human resources at Syracuse China Company. We needed a strong, innovative leader to spearhead our plant safety program and Steve brought all of the expertise and leadership qualities any company would be proud to have on staff. He was exceptional in every respect and his professionalism, knowledge and warm personality made an unmistakable impact from his first day.

So it was not surprising to me when I read this story that Steve would identify a dangerous situation, take immediate and decisive action and end up saving lives.

You see heroes are just ordinary people who rise in the moment to do extraordinary things.

What a lesson Steve gives all of us as leaders. The most potent perhaps is being prepared to serve – having a mindset 24-7 that is wired to serve others before self. We talk in training sessions about the servant-leader as the pinnacle of professional development yet many people struggle to understand the concept of leading through service.

Servant-leadership isn't subservient leadership; it isn't abdicating responsibility but rather embracing it and focusing your talents so completely that your actions are not forced or scripted but simply a reflection of your nature, of a commitment to do the right thing all the time, every time.

That's Steve Valentine's brand of leadership.

You see, in a situation measured in seconds, you don't have time to sort out options, ponder pros and cons of involvement or consider what's in it for you. In situations defined by the split second, you get no second chances.

For leaders like Steve who are the ultimate servant-leaders, there is no thinking, there is only an instinct to act and the courage to execute.

Even driving his family down the interstate, Steve was prepared to serve.

How prepared are you? How committed are you to becoming a servant-leader?

The actions Steve took were exceptionally brave but he would be the first to tell you that what he did was not heroic. He would be the first to shrug off the waves of praise that now rightfully accompany his deed and say that he did what anyone who recognized the need would have done. Steve is a humble man and that is another of his outstanding leadership qualities and another lesson for all of us as leaders.

For the servant-leader, it is always about something bigger than self.

Driver after driver sped by the weaving van and left the lives of a mother and daughter hanging on a prayer until one man answered it.

Steve had the vision to see the need, the courage to act in the moment and the humility to know that he was put on that road at that spit second of his life to make a difference for someone else.

The lesson for us as leaders is to realize we are all called to that same duty – a different road but a common purpose.

Whose hero will you be today?

Judgments prevent us
from seeing the good
that lies beyond
appearances.

Wayne Dyer

Lesson 10: Best Teacher I Ever Had

Mrs. Thompson taught 5th grade and liked to think of herself as a very good teacher who treated all her students the same – that is, until a frumpy little boy named, Teddy Stoddard, sat slumped in a front row seat one year and changed everything.

Mrs. Thompson had watched Teddy the year before and noticed that he didn't play well with the other children, that his clothes were messy, that he constantly needed a bath, and that in fact, Teddy could be very unpleasant. It got to the point where Mrs. Thompson would actually take delight in marking his papers with a broad red pen, making bold X's and then putting a big "F" at the top of his papers.

All that changed though when Mrs. Thompson finally got around to reviewing Teddy's school records.

Teddy's first grade teacher wrote, "Teddy is a bright child with a ready laugh. He does his work neatly and has good manners...he is a joy to be around." His second grade teacher wrote, "Teddy is an excellent student, well liked by his classmates, but he is troubled because his mother has a terminal illness and life at home must be a struggle."

His third grade teacher wrote, "His mother's death has been hard on him. He tries to do his best, but his father doesn't show much interest and his home life will soon affect him if some steps aren't taken." Teddy's fourth grade teacher wrote, "Teddy is withdrawn and doesn't show much interest in school. He doesn't have many friends and sometimes sleeps in class."

Mrs. Thompson realized that Teddy was not a problem child at all but a child whose problems had overwhelmed him. She was ashamed of herself for her haste to judge the struggling boy. She felt even worse when her students brought her Christmas presents that year, wrapped in beautiful paper and tied with pretty ribbons, except for Teddy's, whose present was clumsily wrapped in the heavy, brown paper that he got from a grocery bag.

Opening Teddy's gift, she extracted a rhinestone bracelet with some of the stones missing, and a bottle that was one quarter full of perfume. The other children erupted in laughter but she stifled them with an exclamation of how pretty the bracelet was as she put it on, dabbing some of the perfume on her wrist too. Teddy Stoddard stayed after school that day just long enough to say, "Mrs. Thompson, today you smelled just like my mom used to."

Mrs. Thompson went back to her room, closed the door and cried for an hour. When she composed herself, she vowed to quit teaching reading, and writing, and arithmetic and start teaching children – starting with Teddy. As she worked with him, his mind seemed to come alive. The more she encouraged him, the faster he responded. By the end of the year, Teddy had become one of the smartest children in the class and one of her favorites.

About a year later, Mrs. Thompson walked into her classroom and found a note from Teddy slid under her door. It said that she was still the best teacher he ever had in his whole life. Six years would go by before she got another note from Teddy who wrote that he had finished high school, third in his class, and she was still the best teacher he ever had in his whole life. Four years after that, she got another letter, saying that while things had been tough at times, he'd stayed in school, had stuck with it, and would soon graduate from college with the highest of honors. He assured Mrs. Thompson that she was still the best and favorite teacher he ever had in his whole life.

Four more years passed and yet another letter came explaining that after he got his bachelor's degree, he decided to go a little further. The letter said that she was still the best and favorite teacher he ever had but that now his name was a little longer - the letter was signed, Theodore F. Stoddard, MD.

Later that same spring, there was yet another letter from Teddy saying he was going to be married. He explained that his father had died a couple of years ago and he was wondering if Mrs. Thompson might agree to sit in the place at the wedding that was usually reserved for the mother of the groom.

Mrs. Thompson arrived at the ceremony wearing the bracelet with several rhinestones missing that Teddy had given her so many years before and the perfume that Teddy remembered his mother wearing on their last Christmas together.

They hugged each other, and Dr. Stoddard whispered, "Thank you Mrs. Thompson for believing in me. Thank you so much for making me feel important and showing me that I could make a difference."

Mrs. Thompson, with tears in her eyes, whispered back, "Teddy, you have it all wrong. You were the one who taught me that I could make a difference. I didn't know how to teach until I met you."

"I didn't know how to teach until I met you"
is a phrase many of us can relate to in terms of leadership.

Looking back on our careers, it is easy to identify that one person or one team that had a transformative effect on how we lead people today. Like Mrs. Thompson, it is more often than not the person or team we least expected to have that kind of impact and yet the influence is unmistakable – leaving us better for the experience.

Judgments in haste are dangerous, especially when it comes to people. Initial impressions or unfounded assumptions can take us down a destructive path as leaders and undermine our effectiveness. Our focus is to lift people up when they are down – not to carry them but to give them time to get back on their feet and meet their responsibilities. When we take time to learn about those we lead and let them learn about us, we strengthen our leadership potential.

Leadership is not the power to demand; it is the power to discover.

Just as we can look back and find the "Teddy Stoddard" in our careers, we can also identify the "Mrs. Thompson" – that person who was "the best teacher we ever had". It might be a parent, a sibling, a teacher, a coach, a colleague, a boss, a friend but we know who that person is that took the time to make us better.

What an honor that is to be remembered in such a way.

It's a reminder for us to work everyday at being that person that those we lead now will look back years later and say, "he/she was the best leader I ever worked for."

The story of Dr. Stoddard is an example of the power of pushing past our initial impressions and bias to discover the reality behind the people we lead – what makes them tick and why and how we can use that knowledge to inspire the best from them – and in the process rediscover the best in ourselves.

What we call failure
is not the falling down,
but the staying down.

Mary Pickford

Lesson 11: Gift of Failure

Excerpt from J.K. Rowling, author of the Harry Potter series, Harvard Commencement Address (6-5-08)

"… What I feared most for myself at your age was not poverty, but failure. At your age, in spite of a distinct lack of motivation at university, where I had spent far too long in the coffee bar writing stories, and far too little time at lectures, I had a knack for passing examinations, and that, for years, had been the measure of success in my life and that of my peers.

I am not dull enough to suppose that because you are young, gifted and well-educated, you have never known hardship or heartbreak. Talent and intelligence never yet inoculated anyone against the caprice of the Fates, and I do not for a moment suppose that everyone here has enjoyed an existence of unruffled privilege and contentment.

However, the fact that you are graduating from Harvard suggests that you are not very well-acquainted with failure. You might be driven by a fear of failure quite as much as a desire for success. Indeed, your conception of failure might not be too far from the average person's idea of success, so high have you already flown academically.

Ultimately, we all have to decide for ourselves what constitutes failure, but the world is quite eager to give you a set of criteria if you let it. So I think it fair to say that by any conventional measure, a mere seven years after my graduation day, I had failed on an epic scale.

An exceptionally short-lived marriage had imploded, and I was jobless, a lone parent, and as poor as it is possible to be in modern Britain, without being homeless. The fears my parents had had for me, and that I had had for myself, had both come to pass, and by every usual standard, I was the biggest failure I knew.

Now, I am not going to stand here and tell you that failure is fun. That period of my life was a dark one, and I had no idea that there was going to be what the press has since represented as a kind of fairy tale resolution. I had no idea how far the tunnel extended, and for a long time, any light at the end of it was a hope rather than a reality.

So why do I talk about the benefits of failure? Simply because failure meant a stripping away of the inessential. I stopped pretending to myself that I was anything other than what I was, and began to direct all my energy into finishing the only work that mattered to me. Had I really succeeded at anything else, I might never have found the determination to succeed in the one arena I believed I truly belonged. I was set free, because my greatest fear had already been realized, and I was still alive, and I still had a daughter whom I adored, and I had an old typewriter and a big idea. And so rock bottom became the solid foundation on which I rebuilt my life.

You might never fail on the scale I did, but some failure in life is inevitable. It is impossible to live without failing at something, unless you live so cautiously that you might as well not have lived at all – in which case, you fail by default.

Failure gave me an inner security that I had never attained by passing examinations. Failure taught me things about myself that I could have learned no other way. I discovered that I had a strong will, and more discipline than I had suspected; I also found out that I had friends whose value was truly above rubies.

The knowledge that you have emerged wiser and stronger from setbacks means that you are, ever after, secure in your ability to survive. You will never truly know yourself, or the strength of your relationships, until both have been tested by adversity. Such knowledge is a true gift, for all that it is painfully won, and it has been worth more to me than any qualification I ever earned.

Given a time machine, I would tell my 21-year-old self that personal happiness lies in knowing that life is not a check-list of acquisition or achievement. Your qualifications, your CV, are not your life, though you will meet many people of my age and older who confuse the two. Life is difficult, and complicated, and beyond anyone's total control, and the humility to know that will enable you to survive its vicissitudes."

"Failure taught me things about myself that I could have learned no other way." For us as leaders, failure is the ultimate teacher and invites us to become the ultimate student in its presence. We must balance the humility of knowing that much is outside our control with the confidence in ourselves to tackle what others may see as impossible.

Wisdom is the residue of failure

for those whose vision is sharp enough to see it and whose character is bold enough to embrace it.

J.K. Rowling fell down in her life – over and over. But she refused to stay down, eventually ignoring the soothsayers of doom and committing herself to a course of action that she had a passion for. It was a decision that would lead her to become one of the most successful authors in the world.

Adversity did not limit her, it empowered her; it did not slow her it accelerated her; it did not deter her it inspired her. These are the lessons of failure and the insights we need as leaders.

Courage is fearing the consequences of your inaction more than you fear the potential failure of your own actions. Leaders don't let the fear of failure paralyze them; they know failure is a constant companion of those who push the limits of what is possible. To the shallow, uncommitted cynic, failure is falling down; to a leader, failure is not standing back up.

Adversity is the forge life uses to toughen our mettle but only if we do not fear the flames.

In our own work, how often do we avoid taking action because we fear failing? The pressure to succeed in our culture is so great that it actually limits our success. Today, we must win, win now and win every time or we are labeled a failure – often and ironically, by those who do not even participate in the process.

As leaders, we need to ensure our team does not choose the path of least resistance over the best course of action because they fear falling short. What messages do we convey about how we tolerate failure? How do we reinforce the right effort even if it is occasionally not the right answer?

J.K. Rowling found a magic in Harry Potter that set the world ablaze with imagination.

But as she herself reminds us, the real magic was not in transforming a young wizard into a champion of good over evil but rather in transforming the author from a victim of adversity into its master.

It's a true-life story that's better than the fiction; one that shows us all the gift of failure when we embrace its lessons and accept its challenges.

We are all on a life long journey and the core of its meaning, the terrible demand of its centrality is forgiving and being forgiven.

Martha Kilpatrick

Lesson 12: The Bag

A group of top executives at a large corporation in Texas were not working effectively together. There was infighting and back-biting and turf wars filled with ego and manipulation that left company morale devastated and productivity waning. These senior leaders often undermined each other to the point that the atmosphere at the company had become almost toxic.

Not surprisingly, a new CEO was brought in with orders to clean up the mess. It did not take long for the new chief executive to hire a seasoned business coach to teach her senior team how to work better with each other.

The CEO's directive to her dysfunctional leaders was blunt, "Participate fully and willingly in the training or find a new job."

The executives walked into their first meeting with their new coach to find the tables arranged in a horseshoe around a large, dark green plastic can with a lid firmly in place – the kind you would use for trash or leaves. The leaders took their seats and after some initial introductions the coach asked each of them to spread out around the room.

After they had scattered, the coach asked each to write out a list of any injustice that had been done to them; any issue that had nagged at them as unfair; the names of every person who they felt had wronged them in any way. The coach was very emphatic in urging the executives to make a complete list – leave nothing out, no matter how big or small the issue.

Almost all the executives compiled a very long list.

The coach then distributed one clear plastic garbage bag to each of the executives.

With puzzled stares coming from all his participants, the coach walked into the center of the room and removed the lid from the large plastic can. Inside were clean but unpeeled potatoes.

The coach then instructed the executives to take one potato for each name or situation on their list and to write on the potato the specific offender or injustice. They were then to place it in their clear plastic bag. The executives soon finished with most of the bags being very full and heavy.

Then, the coach directed that the executives carry their bag of potatoes with them everywhere they went for the next two weeks – to meetings, in their car, at their desk, around the house, next to their bed at night, absolutely everywhere – no exceptions. The coach said that there were valuable lessons to be taught in this exercise; ones that would become apparent quickly.

For two weeks, wherever each executive went, his or her plastic bag of potatoes had to go with them.

At first, the executives thought it was funny lugging around a large bag of potatoes but soon the laughter subsided as hassle and embarrassment set in. Everyone noticed these senior leaders hauling around clear bags of spoiling spuds – it was impossible not to gawk.

Day after day, the bags became more of an impediment to their jobs and their lives. The hot, humid Texas sun beating down on the bags as they went back and forth to work added another element of unpleasantness as it did not take long for the potatoes to transform into a smelly, slimy mess.

Two weeks later, the group reconvened with their coach. She explained that the demise of the potatoes represented how quickly such dead-weight in our lives becomes toxic and ugly and how fatiguing it is to carry with us the pain and negativity of things in the past. The coach told them how forgiveness was probably not something they associated with leadership but that when we carry around yesterday's gripes we limit what we can accomplish today. She added that they may have seen forgiveness as a gesture they extended to someone else but that its true value was much deeper.

> In reality, forgiveness is a gift we give ourselves … a freedom to discard that which is no longer healthy or positive in our life.

At the coach's urging, each leader stepped forward and dropped their bag of rotten potatoes into the large trash receptacle; walking away lighter in their burden and with a new appreciation for the power of letting go.

How many of us are carrying around a rotten sack of potatoes full of past injustices, inequities, wrongs, offenses and insults that were perpetrated on us either innocently or maliciously?

How heavy and toxic has that become?

Leaders are champions of the future, not archivists of the past. They accept that bad things happen to good people; that life is not fair; that we are too often the recipient of acts or actions we do not deserve but that none of this is an excuse to fail. Leaders don't ignore negative realities; they deal with them and move on. They understand that to stay mired in the past is to jeopardize the future; that they must avoid the paralysis that comes with thinking or acting like a victim in the face of adversity.

Leaders know others are counting on their strength and vision and watching how they react to unfair situations.

The capacity to forgive is a rare quality that few leaders ever master but that offers enormous strength, wisdom and transformative power. When extended to someone, it is the foundation of a second chance, the fuel for a comeback, the spark to any recovery. It can and has changed the world as many of our greatest leaders were the benefactor of a second chance.

But its real impact is in what it does for us – personally. True forgiveness is not forgetting an injustice or pretending something didn't happen; it is not apathy or sympathy. It is a choice we make – a choice that we have better uses for our energy, talent and life than carrying around the dead-weight of yesterday's pain. Forgiveness is choosing to serve a greater good in our life and in the lives of others. When we do that, tremendous things can happen.

I know because today is August 10th.

On this date years ago, my pregnant wife, Cynthia, died as she drove home from work when a man high on drugs and out to sell his poison ran a stop sign at high speed. There are not words to describe that tragedy but worse still would have been to allow that nightmare to consume my life, my son's life and those around us. I made a conscious choice to acknowledge my grief, anger and fear but then walk away from it and focus instead on serving a greater good.

I have shared "Conquering Adversity" at conferences and special events across the country for thousands of people. At every venue, I am asked how it is that I can deliver such a life-changing message when the roots of the story touch such tragic nerves. The answer is that I believe that at least one person in that room needs my message about the hero inside each of us and that if they were the only person attending I would come and share what I have learned about moving through change, challenge or crisis with them. I believe that my message makes a difference in people's lives so sharing "Conquering Adversity" is how I practice forgiveness; it is how I keep from picking up anger, grief and fear that are persistent hitchhikers on any journey through tragedy.

Forgiveness reminds us to set down the bag of potatoes we all carry, the bag filled with the people and times that have wounded our mind, heart or soul; set the bag down and walk away from yesterday's toxins and free yourself to excel today.

Count blessings, not tears – life is full of both.

Closing Thoughts

Leadership is not a top-down impulse but rather a bottom-up impact. The greatest leaders in history have not been dictators but rather directors – leadership maestros who used their gifts of vision, values and purpose to orchestrate actions that served a cause greater than themselves.

Giving orders is not leadership. Giving hope is. The leader who serves the interest of those he/she leads earns far more than the obedience of their followers, they earn their respect.

Are you an inspired leader? It is good to reflect on how well we are living up to our own leadership challenges. How well are you serving your team and your organization? When was the last time you asked the people you lead how well you are meeting their professional needs? When was the last time that you took a few minutes to sit with each of your team members and asked them what you can do better to help them be more effective or more satisfied in their work? Have you ever asked your colleagues how you can inspire them to excel? Go ahead, ask the questions and do not fear the answers.

Inspired leadership is not about weak and strong; it's about right and wrong. It's about doing things the right way, for the right reasons and using your position of power, trust and influence to serve. Serve as a facilitator to get things done. Serve as a mentor to grow your team members.

Ultimately, the most inspired leaders serve as an example to others that the pinnacle of leadership is reached when you care more about others standing atop the summit than you do about your own view.

The Author

Christopher Novak is an author, professional speaker and leadership coach whose rare combination of experience, empathy and energy make him a sought-after speaker and trainer. As a keynote presenter, he has inspired thousands of people nationally and internationally with his riveting "Conquering Adversity" message. Based on his book, this powerful, true-life presentation focuses on the hero inside each of us and what it takes to rise above change, challenge and adversity in our professional and personal lives.

To bring Christopher Novak to your next event, please contact him at:

Phone: (315) 673-1323
E-mail: info@summit-team.com
Website: www.ConqueringAdversity-speaker.com

The Publisher

For over 30 years, WalkTheTalk.com has been dedicated to one simple goal…one single mission: To provide you and your organization with high-impact resources for your personal and professional success.

Walk The Talk resources are designed to:

- Develop your skills and confidence
- Inspire your team
- Create customer enthusiasm
- Build leadership skills
- Stretch your mind
- Handle tough "people problems"
- Develop a culture of respect and responsibility

Inspired to Lead

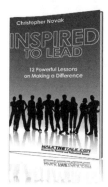

1-24 copies	**$12.95**
25-99 copies	**$11.95**
100-499 copies	**$10.95**
500 + please call	**888.822.99255**

Better yet, consider the Inspired to Lead Kit!

ONLY $34.95

3 best-selling Leadership books packed with practical, tactical and inspirational leadership strategies!

- **Inspired To Lead** - 12 Powerful Leadership Lessons
- **Lead Right** - Straight-Talk Strategies for Leadership Success
- **212° the extra degree** - The Message that's Motivating Millions!

For more information, or to order these or other
Walk The Talk Resources, please visit **www.walkthetalk.com**
or call **800.888.2811** (972.899.8300)

Visit

WALKTHETALK.COM

Resources for Personal and Professional Success

To Learn More About Our...

Leadership and Employee Development Centre

- Develop your Leaders
- Build Employee Commitment
- Achieve Business Results

Free Newsletters

- Daily Inspiration
- The Power of Inspiration
- The Leadership Solution
- Inspired Living

Motivational Gift Books

- Inspire your Team
- Create Customer Enthusiasm
- Reinforce Core Values